FOLLOW THE KING

MODELS FOR HEROIC LIVING

Jaroslav Vajda

Publishing House
St. Louis

Photos by: Bruce Roberts—13, 68, 81; Ted Laatsch—21; H. Armstrong Roberts—32; Adele Pardiech—65; Jim Murphy—77; Ernst Peterson—88

1977 Edition
Concordia Publishing House, St. Louis, Missouri

MANUFACTURED IN THE UNITED STATES OF AMERICA

Library of Congress Cataloging in Publication Data

Vajda, Jaroslav.
Follow the King.

Edition for 1964 published under title: They followed the King.
1. Bible—Biography. I. Title.
BS571.V28 1977 220.9'2 [B] 76-30651
ISBN 0-570-03049-8

To my Wife Louise

CONTENTS

INTRODUCTION

Faith, like love, is "a many-splendored thing." It cannot be described in one word or with just one picture. One has to look at it from many sides to get a glimpse of its glory.

Still, faith is just one thing. It is the sinner taking hold of the life and death of God's Son and holding on for *all* of his help and life. This every child of God possesses. How large faith is does not matter for salvation. It is either there or it isn't. Where it exists, there is forgiveness received, and the door of heaven is open.

In some people of God the grasp of the new life in Christ is stronger than in others. This does not mean that they are more saved than the weak believers. It does mean that the new life that follows faith does more for God and their fellowmen, and it does more for their life here on earth.

Faith, though unseen except to the eyes of God, shows itself by various virtues. Extraordinary trust in God, patience, courage, love, loyalty, purity, and long-suffering are some of the gifts of grace available to believers. Not all these virtues are present in the same quantity in all believers. In some, one or more of these virtues are outstanding. These are the heroes of faith.

In these pages we shall observe and frankly admire how faith responds to the grace of God. The vessels are all made of clay, even as you and I, but the power poured into them continues to amaze us. Let this "cloud of witnesses" testify to us how strong faith can be and what God can do with the believer.

ABEL

By faith Abel offered unto God a more excellent sacrifice than Cain.

Heb. 11:4

The Kind of Sacrifice God Accepts

Not for a long time did God spell out for His creatures the sacrifices they owed Him. And yet Cain and Abel, the first two brothers, brought sacrifices to the Lord. It was something they felt they should do because God was God and they were His creatures.

Each brother took a portion of the product of his occupation: Cain, a vegetable offering from his farmland; Abel, an animal sacrifice from his flocks. The kind of offering each decided to bring made no difference to God. Both kinds were later prescribed by God for His people.

But with Cain and Abel, one offering was acceptable to God, the other was not. This is what led the first human being born on earth to murder the second. There was something behind the sacrifices that God saw, which made one sacrifice acceptable and the other not.

Outwardly they both seemed to be doing the same thing. What could be more wholesome, decent, or desirable than for people to join in a religious service? What better omen was there for the human race than this voluntary, unforced worship? And yet the sacrifice ended in the first murder in history. There must have been some deep division between the brothers that crippled even their act of worship and prevented them from living together in peace and harmony. God puts His finger on the trouble when He says: "By faith Abel offered unto God a more excellent sacrifice than Cain."

Abel may not have known it, but he was running a risk by being faithful. He was inviting the hostility of his unbelieving brother. There, in the first human family, the division of the human race begins. Jesus exposed it when He said to His small band of followers: "If you were of the world, the world would love its own; but because you are not of the world, but I chose you out of the world, therefore the world hates you" (John 15:19 RSV). John reminded the early Christians of what Abel-like faith provokes when he wrote: "We should love one another, and not be like Cain, who was of the evil one and murdered his brother. And why did he murder him? Because his own deeds were evil and his brother's righteous. Do not wonder, brethren, that the world hates you." (1 John 3:11-13 RSV)

Abel might have been safe had he abandoned faith as his brother had and just gone through the motions of worship. If Abel's life had not shone with faith, Cain's evil deeds would not have been shown up, and Cain would not have killed his brother—at least not for that reason. Cain resented the sermon Abel was preaching by merely living. He had to silence that testimony of faith. He thought killing would do it. It didn't stop the voice of Abel's faith. His innocent blood cried to God for vengeance, and his voice goes on speaking to succeeding generations. "He died, but through his faith he is still speaking." (Heb. 11:4 RSV)

What is Abel saying? That it's no use sacrificing to God unless you do it from faith. That God accepts only those sacrifices that come from a broken spirit and a contrite heart. That living or sacrificing without God's approval is futile. That faith divides the human race into two hostile camps. That faith will risk danger and even death to be found among the sheep at the right hand of Christ, to whom the King says: "Come, O blessed of My Father, inherit the kingdom prepared for you from the foundation of the world." (Matt. 25:34)

By faith Abel was the first to stand in that happy company.

NOAH

By faith Noah, being warned by God concerning events as yet unseen, took heed and constructed an ark for the saving of his household; by this he condemned the world and became an heir of the righteousness which comes by faith.

Heb. 11:7 RSV

A Boat on Dry Land

There was old Noah, building a boat on dry land, miles from any water that could possibly float it—if it would float at all.

His neighbors watched him and shook their head. They had wondered about him before, with his different way of living, his criticism of their way, his worship of God. But now they were sure he was unbalanced. Of all the crazy projects!

And the reason he gave for building the monstrous boat seemed even more preposterous. God, he said, told him that the human race would be destroyed for its wickedness. And this destruction was to happen by a flood. But no one began building an ark except Noah.

This man believed that God was really going to destroy mankind. If the warning was true, the danger was still more than a hundred years away. Yet Noah did not wait to see the rain falling before he gathered tools and materials for the construction of the ark. Whether the rest of the world cared or not, Noah wanted to be ready for the rains when they came.

By pursuing this "crazy" project, Noah was preaching a sermon to the rest of the world. Everyone else, except Noah's family, went on as though nothing would change. They saw no reason for leaving their established way of living. Each day seemed to them like the one just past. And there was no water in sight to float anything the size of Noah's boat. By their behavior they indicated that living in unfaith is nothing to be concerned about, that the warnings of punishment for sin are not to be taken seriously. And so they did nothing about the warning.

When God announced the flood to Noah, Noah was not just to drop his head into his hands and bewail the sad plight of the world. He was to get busy investing time, work, and money into building for tomorrow's rescue, like a man building a fallout shelter long before a possible nuclear attack. By expending the effort it takes to build a shelter, a man says something about his faith or his fears.

Every morning when Noah got up, there stood the ark in his backyard reminding him of God's promise and his neighbors of God's warning. The news of such an unusual project would certainly get around. It would attract the attention of the world just as Christians do when they conscientiously prepare for the Day of Judgment. They

NOAH—"And the rains came, and the waters rose, and the ark floated."

plan and act according to their confession in the Creed: "I believe that Jesus Christ will come again to judge the quick and the dead." And they advertise to the world that "ark" by which they expect to be saved.

It wasn't easy for Noah to be such a small minority in the world. All the visible evidence seemed to be on the side of those who mocked the warnings and the provision God had made for rescue. All Noah had to depend on was God's word. And that is where Noah's faith rested.

And the rains came, and the waters rose, and the ark floated, and only Noah and his family were saved!

Exactly as God had said!

JOB

Though He slay me, yet will I trust in Him.
Job 13:15

Not Every Man Has His Price

How far must a man be pushed before he will let go of God?

Many a person has abandoned faith in God for a comparatively small price. Moses was gone from his people on Mount Sinai for a little over a month, and they turned their back on the God who had recently liberated them, preferring the worship of Egyptian idols. To please his pagan wives, Solomon, who once walked with God and erected a magnificent temple to His glory, deserted the familiar paths of faith. Demas, Paul's partner in God's plan for winning the world, forsook the company of God's family for the love of the world. For whatever reason men leave God, the price of their treason is usually quite cheap.

It was different with Job. When Satan took on Job to prove to God what he thought was faith's breaking point, he bit into a harder nut than he imagined.

In this unique test of faith, God permitted Satan to deprive Job of 7,000 sheep, 3,000 camels, 500 yoke of oxen, 500 asses, and numerous servants. It had taken Job many years of diligent work to accumulate such wealth. More crippling to Job, however, were the losses he suffered in his own family, his seven sons and three daughters. Yet even these disasters were not heavy enough to press Job into cursing God. As each piece of earthly ballast was pulled away from Job, he soared higher and closer to God. At this point his outlook was: "The Lord gave, and the Lord hath taken away; blessed be the name of the Lord." (Job 1:21)

Job had lost all but his wife and his friends, but he still had not been touched in his body. Here, Satan thought, Job's price would be found.

"And Satan answered the Lord and said, Skin for skin, yea, all that a man hath will he give for his life. But put forth Thine hand now and touch his bone and his flesh, and he will curse Thee to Thy face." (Job 2:4, 5)

But Satan had underestimated his quarry again. Not even the twisting tortures of a pain-consumed body could pull Job away from God. Neither the disappointment of a despairing wife nor the misunderstanding and unfair accusations of his remaining friends could jar this man loose from his God. With nothing left but a trickle of life, Job would only cry: "Though He slay me, yet will I trust in Him."

What kind of glue holds a man to God like that? Paul, suffering similar slings of Satan, sang the song of Job thus:

"Who shall separate us from the love of Christ? Shall tribulation or distress or persecution or famine or nakedness or peril or sword? As it is written.

"'For Thy sake we are being killed all the day long; we are regarded as sheep to be slaughtered,'

"No, in all these things we are more than conquerors through Him who loved us. For I am sure that neither death nor life, nor angels nor principalities, nor things present nor things to come, nor powers, nor height nor depth, nor anything else in all creation, will be able to separate us from the love of God in Christ Jesus, our Lord." (Rom. 8:35-39 RSV)

By the grace of God, not every man has his price.

ABRAHAM I

By faith Abraham obeyed when he was called to go out to a place which he was to receive as an inheritance; and he went out, not knowing where he was to go.

Heb. 11:8 RSV

Letting God Chart the Course

Life had been pretty good to Abram and His wife Sarai back in Ur of the Chaldeans. They were settled comfortably in the fertile Mesopotamian valley. Abram had accumulated a considerable amount of wealth in cattle, silver, gold, servants, and other possessions. By the time he was 75 years old, Abram might have imagined that the struggles were behind him, that he could now relax and enjoy the fruits of many years' labors. Having no children, he and his wife would have only themselves to care for in their retirement.

God, however, had other plans for this man. Abram was meant to enjoy a different kind of inheritance, an altogether different future from that which he had planned for himself. God had chosen Abram to be the first Hebrew, to become the father of a great nation and numerous descendants, and to be the father of believers. Part of this plan involved moving Abram from Babylonia hundreds of miles west to the land of Canaan.

This order of the Lord was one to make anyone hesitate and wonder, especially someone as advanced in years as was Abram. Elderly people do not adjust to new ideas readily. They are reluctant to forsake extablished patterns and familiar places. Yet this is what God was telling Abram and his wife to do, "Go from your country and your kindred and your father's house to the land that I will show you." (Gen. 12:1 RSV)

Abram was to leave something that was in his hands in favor of something invisible and far away. How could he know it would be better for him in that strange land than it was in his home now? He had taken many a gamble in his life. What reason was there for him to take this one? How could things improve over what he had already? There was, in fact, a good chance that he might lose everything he had gained. He might well become the laughingstock of his friends ("There's no fool like an old fool," they might say), and as for that promise of his becoming a great nation—well, that was even too fantastic to consider!

Though we would expect the average person in Abram's position to say, "No, thank you," the response of Abram sets him apart for all of history and entitles him to special mention in Hebrews 11. In Genesis 12 it is reported: "So Abram went, as the Lord had told him. . . . Abram was seventy-five years old when he departed from Haran . . . and they set forth to go to the land of Canaan." (Gen. 12:4, 5)

The writer of Hebrews comments that it was "by faith [that] Abraham, when he was called to go out into a place which he should after receive for an inheritance, *obeyed;* and he went out, now knowing whither he went" (Heb. 11:8). Abram traded a permanent residence in Haran for a life of tenting, confident that his Navigator knew where He was leading him. "For he looked for a city which hath foundations, whose builder and maker is God." (Heb. 11:10)

So it was that Abram came from the East to the promised land in the West, taking the path of the sun, carrying with him the light of God's grace and becoming a light and life-giving blessing to many future pilgrims by means of the Savior whose day he rejoiced to see.

ABRAHAM II

By faith Abraham, when he was tested, offered up Isaac, and he who had received the promises was ready to offer up his only son, of whom it was said, Through Isaac shall your descendants be named. He considered that God was able to raise men from the dead; hence, figuratively speaking, he did receive him back.

Heb. 11:17-19 RSV

The Ultimate Test

When does a believer stop being tested?

Unquestioningly Abram had accepted the challenge of God to forsake Haran and his home and kindred and travel to far-off Canaan. Charting his course and future only by the word of the Lord, he went.

But God was promising Abram more than just the deed to a country of his own, though that was a large enough gift. "I will make of you a great nation," God tells 75-year-old Abram. This meant that sometime thereafter Abram and Sarai would have to have a son. It was fantastic enough to imagine that Sarai, childless up to this time, would have a child, and ever more miraculous that the one child would be a male.

After this promise was made to Abram, it lay dormant for 25 years. In the meantime, Sarai, impatient with waiting, urged Abram to have a child by her Egyptian maid Hagar, assuming that the child, Ishmael, would serve as the fulfillment of the promise. But this was not the child of promise. This was a child of the flesh, born of the will of man. The promised son was to be a child of both Abram and Sarai. When 90-year-old Sarai heard this, she laughed. But the Lord rebuked her unbelief, saying: "Is anything too hard for the Lord?" (Gen. 18:14)

And then the child was born. To Sarai and to Abram. And it was a boy. And the names of Abram ("Exalted Father") and Sarai were changed to Abraham ("Father of a Multitude") and to Sarah. They had entered the age of fulfilled promise.

But not altogether. Now the question arose: Would this child live, and would he have children?

First, would he live? To make this question even more impossible to answer, God confronted him with still another test of faith. He commanded Abraham to take teen-aged Isaac up to a mountain and sacrifice him to the Lord. This was the ultimate test. If Isaac should die, then there would be no nation, the carrier of the promise would be eliminated, and Abraham's journey to Canaan would have been pointless.

What would Abraham do with this challenge, not only to his faith in God's promise but to his own fatherly feelings of love for his child?

He obeyed the Lord without question. No one but God the Father can know what feelings went through the heart of Abraham as he prepared to sacrifice his only-begotten son. Abraham went ahead with the plans with heavy heart, yet knowing that God would somehow carry out His promise, even if He had to resurrect the slain son. Abraham obeyed, "accounting that God was able to raise him up, even from the dead." (Heb. 11:19)

We know the results of the test. God intervened when

MOSES—". . . faith opened a path for them . . ."

He saw the trust of Abraham. When the test was over, God announced to Abraham: "By Myself I have sworn . . . because you have not withheld your son, your only son, I will indeed bless you . . . because you have obeyed My voice." (Gen. 22:16-18)

Nothing about Abraham was as important to the Lord as his great and enduring faith. Not his wealth or his prestige. But "Abraham believed the Lord; and He reckoned it to him as righteousness" (Gen. 15:6). Abraham passed all the tests, including the ultimate one, that of loving the Lord more than his own son.

Willing to suffer every loss, Abraham gained God, and with God, everything.

MOSES

And there arose not a prophet since in Israel like unto Moses.

Deut. 34:10

"By Faith Moses . . ."

Moses was like a well-equipped army lacking only courage to be victorious. The raw materials that went to make up the man were impressive. He grew up in the palace of the mighty Egyptian Pharaoh. He was educated in the highest wisdom of one of the most advanced cultures in history. He knew his way around the royal court, the intrigues that had to be played, the pressures that could be applied to get what you wanted. He could evaluate the forces of this world power. And during a 40-year exile, Moses learned the wilderness between Egypt and his countrymen's homeland as well as an Indian scout knew the terrain of primitive America.

Only one ingredient had to be applied to this man's outstanding traits and training to make him useful to God in delivering a nation from foreign bondage: and that was faith. Moses had it.

We see how it worked in him to carry out the daring plan of God.

God used Moses' parents to plant the faith in him. "By faith Moses, when he was born, was hid three months of his parents, because they saw that he was a proper child; and they were not afraid of the king's commandment" (Heb. 11:23). This was the first push Moses had in the direction of his destiny. His life would be a constant choosing of the higher alternative, even though each choice would place his life in danger. The first choice of faith was made for Moses by his parents, when they boldly trusted that God would preserve the baby's life against the decree of Pharaoh that all Jewish male children should be killed.

"By faith Moses, when he was come to years, refused to be called the son of Pharaoh's daughter; choosing rather to suffer affliction with the people of God than to enjoy the pleasures of sin for a season; esteeming the reproach of Christ greater riches than the treasures of Egypt; for he had respect unto the recompence of the reward" (Heb. 11:24-26). There came a time when Moses had to choose between the advantage of palace living as an adopted Egyptian or the hazard of identifying himself with his own afflicted people. The allure of the gay court life was strong; the treasures available to him were stunning. But Moses weighed these advantages against the lot of his people and

God's people—and he made the choice of faith, certain that the reward of such a choice would far outweigh what he was giving up personally.

"By faith he forsook Egypt, not fearing the wrath of the king; for he endured, as seeing Him who is invisible" (Heb. 11:27). The king of Egypt and his armed forces were very visible. The shouts of the taskmasters were heard above the cries of the groaning Hebrew slaves. But Moses saw another force, mightier than Egypt's. He heard another voice, more compelling than the oppressor's. Following that Voice and trusting in that Force, Moses chose to defend his oppressed countrymen, and went into exile. The last bridge behind him was burned.

He returned, however, by another bridge, by the bridge of God's promise to deliver His people at all costs. "Through faith he kept the Passover and the sprinkling of blood, lest He that destroyed the firstborn should touch them" (Heb. 11:28). This was the final test of faith for Moses and the Israelites before the doors of their imprisonment would burst open. They had to believe that the smearing of the spotless lamb's blood on their doorposts would preserve them from the visit of the angel of death. And this act of faith, repeated by every child of God who trusts in the blood of God's Lamb on Calvary's cross, was initiated by Moses before the final plague struck.

"By faith they passed through the Red Sea as by dry land; which the Egyptians assaying to do were drowned" (Heb. 11:29). Without faith Moses and the Israelites would have drowned as did the Egyptians when they reached the Red Sea in their flight from slavery. But faith opened a path for them through this obstacle that destroyed the faithless.

Faith changed the timid, stammering shepherd into a

courageous emancipator. Faith saw the plan of God and carried it out. Faith placed all the native abilities and advantages of a favored man into the hands of God and said: Use them to Your glory.

ISAAC

And Isaac said to his father Abraham, My father.
And he said, Here am I, my son.

Gen 22:7 RSV

"The Fear of Isaac"

When do you stop being a child? By the laws of the state, at the age of 18 or 21. In your relationship to God, never.

We are always and forever the children of God. When we know this, we know how it really is between us and God. As long as we live we are to pray: "Our Father." And when we breathe our last, the best prayer our lips can utter is that of the 33-year-old Son of God: "Father, into Thy hands I commend My spirit."

We are out of step with reality when we step out of this Father-son relationship with God. This special relationship is one of complete devotion to the Father, an eagerness to do the will of the Father, and a profound reluctance to displease the Father. No one lived this relationship more perfectly than Jesus.

Isaac was like our Lord in so many filial ways. He was a child by a special promise. He was an only son, greatly loved by his father. He was named by God and circumcised on the eighth day.

As a young man (Josephus estimated Isaac to have been 25 years old), Isaac was led under orders of God by his father to be sacrificed on a mountain. Isaac did not rebel at the maneuverings of his father in that direction. He even carried the wood for his sacrifice up the mountainside and permitted himself to be laid on the altar. There was no doubt in his father's mind that since this was the will of God, God could and would raise his son from the dead, if necessary, to fulfill His promise of the Messiah.

Isaac lived out his life in a Christlike pattern of submissiveness to the Lord's will. He believed that it is God who lays out the plan for our life and that it is up to us to conform to that plan so that God may accomplish His purposes. He showed his respect for God's wisdom by doing the will of God as God wanted it to be done.

Isaac's son Jacob used to recall this special quality of his father and referred to it as the "fear of Isaac." It was the same quality that was so prominent in Isaac's Seed, Jesus, toward His heavenly Father, whom He was determined to obey in the form of a servant even to the death of the cross.

God Himself enjoys such a childlike stance toward Him. He delights in identifying Himself as "the God of Abraham, *Isaac,* and Jacob."

The child is also blessed when he stands in such a relationship toward God. To Isaac's confidential call, "My Father," his father Abraham lovingly responded, "Here am I, my son." When God's children cry, "Abba, Father," "like as a father pitieth his children, so the Lord pitieth them that fear Him." (Ps. 103:13)

There is no warmth or closeness to compare with the love between the heavenly Father and His children. Isaac knew it long before he got to meet the perfect Child of God whose preview he was privileged to be. He preferred never to grow out of God's family.

JACOB

I will not let You go unless You bless me.
Gen. 32:26b RSV

The Limping Hero

There, hard to understand, is the name of Jacob in the 11th chapter of Hebrews. We can readily see why Abraham and Moses are in that select list of heroes—but Jacob? We wonder.

And so we examine the life of the man after whom the Israelites were named to see what was so heroic about it. And what we discover is a limping hero.

Prior to his birth, God had informed his mother that Jacob would rule over his firstborn twin brother Esau. Rebekah favored Jacob and prompted him to deceive his father Isaac to get the birthright. Jacob had already bought the birthright from his brother for a pottage of lentils. With and without encouragement, Jacob obtained the advantages he wanted honestly or by craft. When he set his heart on something, he permitted nothing to stand in his way. He would sacrifice or cheat, work or wrestle for what he wanted.

It took him 14 years of hard labor to get the wife he wanted. He had to struggle against the treachery of his uncle Laban and suffer the kind of deceit he himself had practiced. Finally he broke away to go to his homeland, a rich and prosperous man. He had wanted much and he had obtained much. Most other men would have been satisfied long before they achieved what Jacob had.

But not Jacob. All that he had received in the way of material possessions would fall out of his hands one day. All this he would leave behind. There was one blessing, however, that he simply had to have above all others.

And then, one day, on his return to Canaan, Jacob was left standing all alone. He had sent his family on ahead to be safe in case Esau would be unforgiving and would kill him. That night Jacob wrestled with an unknown adversary until the break of day. As in every other effort, Jacob was determined to win. He would not let go of the man even when the man threw Jacob's thigh out of joint.

"I will not let You go," said Jacob, "unless You bless me." At this the man asked Jacob: "What is your name?" And he answered: "Jacob." Then the stranger said: "Your name shall no more be called Jacob, but Israel [He who strives with God], for you have striven with God and with men and have prevailed." And there He blessed Jacob. "So Jacob called the name of the place Peniel [The face of God], saying, 'For I have seen God face to face, and yet my life is preserved.' The sun rose upon him as he passed Penuel, limping because of his thigh." (Gen. 32:28-32)

Jacob must have wanted very badly what only God could give him. That coveted blessing meant more to him than all he could gain by his own efforts and scheming. It was like a Holy Grail before him, in his dreams and in his heart. No one can approve of the weaknesses and methods of Jacob in getting what he wanted. But he can be envied for his consuming obsession with the gracious blessing of God.

Some gifts have to be wrestled and prayed out of the hand of God. There is some of the heroism of Jacob in every believer who will not leave a visit in God's house or stand up from his prayers unless he can depart with the Lord's blessing.

As we watch Jacob limping off into the sunrise, we see how badly a man can want what only God can give.

DAVID I

I come to you in the name of the Lord of hosts.
1 Sam. 17:45 RSV

That Mighty Majority of One

Booming across the Valley of Elah came the bloodcurdling boasts of Goliath, the Philistine champion. Towering some ten feet high, armed with heavy mail, and brandishing a spear the size of a weaver's beam, the spectacular giant of Gath roared at the cringing Israelites: "I defy the ranks of Israel this day; give me a man that we may fight together" (1 Sam. 17:10). No response came from King Saul and his warriors except the sound of shaking knees and fluttering hearts.

The odds were impossible. Nowhere in the forces of Israel was there a man to match the strength and size of Goliath. The giant had many a notch in his lance to remind them of the foolish foes who dared take up his challenges. And yet, unless the Israelites came up with someone to fight the Philistine, they were in danger of losing their independence, their country, and, quite possibly, their lives.

The fact was Goliath had an equal on the other side whom few of the Israelites remembered in this dark hour. They should have remembered. He had won many a victory for them in the past, sometimes single-handed against enemies stronger than the Philistines. But they had forgotten. They felt that now they were on their own. This challenge seemed different. Now they were a nation like others, with armies and a king. Now they expected to fight their own battles alone in the only way nations know: with superior skill and armor. But they simply didn't have it. And that is why they waited for the onslaught paralyzed with fear.

One person in Israel remembered their superior advantage. When he was older, he recorded that advantage in songs to be recited over and over again: "The Lord is the Strength of my life; of whom shall I be afraid?" (Ps. 27:1). "Be of good courage, and He shall strengthen your heart, all ye that hope in the Lord." (Ps. 31:24)

Israel was at the point of a drowning man clutching at a straw. If they were going to be beaten anyway, why not give David a chance? Yet even now they weren't ready to go as far as David in their trust in God. They would load him down with the bulky armor in which they had been placing so much of their confidence.

David took off the armor, chose five stones from a brook, grasped his shepherd's staff, and unwound his sling. Then he strode out into that empty valley. Invisibly Someone else walked alongside. David felt Him there. "The Lord is my Shepherd. . . . Though I walk through the valley of the shadow of death, I will fear no evil; for Thou are with me; Thy rod and Thy staff, they comfort me" (Ps. 23:1, 4). The Lord made him audacious.

Once more the giant laughed at the ridiculous sight—and then fell dead with a stone embedded in his skull.

Come, little David, play on your harp, and sing hallelujah! It can be done. Any odds can be faced, every foe can be beaten—with the arm of the Lord!

How would David have said it?

"If it had not been the Lord who was on our side, now may Israel say: if it had not been the Lord who was on our side, when men rose up against us; then they had swallowed us up quick, when their wrath was kindled against us; then the waters had overwhelmed us, the streams had gone over our soul; then the proud waters had gone over our soul. Blessed be the Lord, who hath not given us as a prey to their teeth. Our soul is escaped as a bird out of the snare of the fowlers; the snare is broken, and we are escaped. Our help is in the name of the Lord, who made heaven and earth." (Ps. 124)

DAVID II

I have found David, the son of Jesse, a man after Mine own heart, which shall fulfill all My will.
Acts 13:22

Big Man—Big Influence

If Lord Acton's dictum is true, that "power tends to corrupt, and absolute power corrupts absolutely," then the man in high places who walks humbly before his God is a rare creature indeed.

Looking over the index of the world's great, we do not find many who have successfully overcome the hazard to worship power or to use it only for their own advantage.

Even among the Bible's listing of strong men, only a few are said to be men "after the Lord's own heart." Solomon doesn't make the roll call of heroes in Hebrews 11, nor does Nebuchadnezzar or Ahab or Alexander the Great or any of the Roman emperors or any of the Ptolemies of Egypt. But there is David's name.

Give the average man unusual power or prestige, and watch him change his values, puff up with pride, and trample others in his drive for the top. Even very few Christians can stand off the temptations that come with riches and power. Knowing the hazards of wealth, Jesus warned His disciples: "Verily, I say unto you, That a rich man shall hardly enter into the kingdom of heaven. And again I say unto you, It is easier for a camel to go through the eye of a needle than for a rich man to enter into the kingdom of God." (Matt. 19:23, 24)

David successfully overcame this temptation to consider himself the lord of his own life just because he was lord over others. He remembered his early shepherd life, out of which he was chosen by God to be anointed king of Israel. The Lord was his Shepherd; David was always the sheep reposing in the Shepherd's arm.

David remembered also that the Lord was his Deliverer as He was the Deliverer of His people from the hand of the Philistines and Goliath. Though great and mighty enemies fell before his arms, David acknowledged privately and publicly that it was the arm of the Lord that had gotten him the victory.

David remembered that he had not selected himself to be king, nor did he fight his way to the throne of Israel.

DAVID—". . . the streams had gone over our soul."

The kingdom fell into his lap. And all because the Lord had His eye on David and considered David a man after His own heart. The Lord liked the way David submitted himself to God's will, how he delighted in the Lord, how he recognized the grace of God in choosing him, how he loved the Law of the Lord, how he longed for the coming of the Messiah. This man was a model ruler, a man who would use his great influence for the good of many.

Like all saints, David was also a sinner. In wrongdoing he is, of course, not to be imitated. David himself suffered anguish and punishment for it, and regretted it deeply. He was torn apart by remorse and sincerely repented of his transgression, feeling bad not that he had been caught and judged for sinning, but that he had disobeyed and offended his loving Lord. "Against Thee, Thee only, have I sinned and done this evil in Thy sight," he wept. Many a sleepless night he was troubled by his conscience.

And then he rose from the depths of contrition to say with confidence: "I acknowledged my sin unto Thee, and mine iniquity have I not hid. I said, I will confess my transgressions unto the Lord; and Thou forgavest the iniquity of my sin." (Ps. 32:5)

What a man! What a believer! What a child of God! No wonder that God delighted to call David His servant! Here was an example to the world of what a ruler could be. God could accomplish His purposes in a man like this. God could use a man like this to preview the glorious kingdom of Christ.

Millions venerate David as a mighty man, a historical hero. His star is displayed proudly by a proud nation. Millions have thanked God for the gift of David the psalmist and prophet. But the best accolade of all is that of the Lord, who said: "I have found David a man after Mine own heart."

CALEB

But My servant Caleb, because he has a different spirit and has followed Me fully, I will bring into the land into which he went, and his descendants shall possess it.

Num. 14:24 RSV

The Minority Report

The majority isn't always right. Though it carries the weight of numbers, it can be very blind to the facts. Caleb knew this and acted accordingly.

The Children of Israel had been on the march from Egypt for a comparatively short time. They had arrived near the border of the Promised Land. Before proceeding to their goal, God directed Moses to dispatch 12 spies into the land to find out the strength of the squatters occupying His people's inheritance. Each of the spies was the chief man of his tribe.

The 12 went, disguised, through the land of their fathers for 40 days. They were amazed at what they saw. Some of the evidence they were able to bring back: a cluster of grapes so huge it took two men to carry it. For the rest of the report the Israelites would have to rely on the observations of the spies and their considered conclusions.

The 12, however, were not unanimous in their report. They had all seen the same things, but they were of two conflicting opinions.

Ten of the spies stood before the assembled refugees and presented their report. "The land flows with milk and honey, but its inhabitants are dreadfully strong. We seemed like grasshoppers compared with them," they whined. It was a report completely lacking in confidence. Nevertheless it carried with the people. They were ready to accept the fearful conclusions of the 10. The minority report could hardly be heard above the lamentation. "All the congregation raised a loud cry; and the people wept that night. And all the people of Israel murmured against Moses and Aaron. . . . And they said to one another, 'Let us choose a captain and go back to Egypt.'" (Num. 14:1, 2, 4, RSV)

To forestall the revolt, Joshua and Caleb, the two remaining spies, pleaded with the nation to reconsider its decision. "If the Lord delights in us," they said, "He will bring us into this land and give it to us. . . . The Lord is with us; do not fear them." They got nowhere. Rather, "all the congregation said to stone them with stones." (Num. 14:8-10 RSV)

The people were ready to abandon their journey on into the Land of Promise. But Caleb could not see it. They had been brought this far so that they might inherit the land of Canaan. The situation looked entirely different to Caleb than it did to the 10 spies. The longer he compared the forces opposing Israel with the proved might of the Lord, the more they shrank in size and terror.

Caleb's name happens to mean "bold" or "dog." It couldn't have fit him better. Like a dog he clamped his teeth on his objective, tussled with it and shook it, and would not let go. Doggedly he kept insisting that they would win with the Lord. Let the others go back to Egypt or into the barren wilderness, he was for plunging ahead, counting on the Lord's faithfulness to His people.

The majority did return to the wilderness, but Caleb made it to the Promised Land—some 40 years later. God condemned Israel to wandering in the wilderness outside its homeland's boundaries for the number of years equal to the number of days spent by the spies in Canaan. Of all who had left Egypt above the age of 20, not one would enter the Promised Land except Caleb and that other member of the minority, Joshua.

The majority left their bones in the wilderness and their names in oblivion. The majority wasn't right after all. The truth was on the side of those who looked at the facts through the eyes of faith.

JOSHUA

By faith the walls of Jericho fell down after they had been encircled for seven days.

Heb. 11:30 RSV

"The Walls Come Tumblin' Down"

For seven days Joshua and his people walked around their problem. On the seventh day thay walked around it seven times. This was no desperate pacing about, looking for a way out of a hopeless situation. This marching of Israel around Jericho was an act of faith, a hopeful anticipation of a solution to their problem. On the seventh day their "problem" collapsed in dust before them. It is written that their faith caused the walls to fall down.

Under the leadership of Moses the Children of Israel had been trained for 40 years for this critical hour at the borders of the Holy Land. Each day of those four decades they had to depend on the providential care of God. A wandering nation of two million refugees has a great many needs. At the beginning of their long journey God said to them: "Behold, I will rain bread from heaven for you; and the people shall go out and gather a day's portion every day" (Ex. 16:4 RSV). And at the end of the journey He told them: "I have led you forty years in the wilderness; your clothes have not worn out upon you, and your sandals have not worn off your feet." (Deut. 29:5 RSV)

Over and over again during that time God had delivered them out of the grasp of superior forces. Fierce enemies had been swept before them. And they knew it was not their own prowess but the arm of the Lord which had gotten them the victory.

Even the obstacles of nature had been removed for them in miraculous ways. The Red Sea opened a path for them, water gushed forth in the desert, and poisonous snakes were driven out of their camp. And the Lord's hand was behind it all.

Now they stood at the very boundaries of the land their forefathers had left 470 years earlier. Before them lay the fields and vineyards "flowing with milk and honey." All they had to do was reach out and possess the land.

One final barrier barred the way to the land of promise. Just across the Jordan, which parted for them as did the Red Sea, rose the formidable walls of Jericho. Weapons had not yet been invented which could demolish those defenses. If they were to try to take the city themselves, they would run the risk of depleting a large part of their manpower. They might even be prevented from advancing beyond this point. Only those wall separated them from their goal and dream, freedom and promise. But what walls they were!

God had not brought them this far to desert then now.

He would continue to fight their battles for them. He told Joshua, the successor of Moses, that He would remove that final barrier for them. They were to march around the city once each day for seven days, and seven times on the seventh day, and at the sound of the trumpets, to shout.

Joshua had just taken over the leadership of the nation. Now he had to make a decision that would affect his subsequent leadership among the people. He could either follow these "unbelievable" directives of the Lord and let the Lord take the city and the credit for the victory, or he could substitute a plan of his own in which his own military skill would shine and, IF the city could be taken, make a name for himself.

Without hesitation, Joshua relayed the orders God had given him. They would take the city—with the help of God. Like the other "Joshua" (even the name is the same—Joshua, Jesus) who came centuries later, this Joshua's motto was, "My food is to do the will of Him who sent me, and to accomplish His work" (John 4:34 RSV). Like that greater "Joshua" he would lead God's people into the land of promise by faith in the One who made the promise.

The faith of Joshua inspired the people to similar faith, and "the people shouted, and the trumpets were blown . . . and the wall fell down flat so that the people went up into the city, every man straight before him, and they took the city." (Joshua 6:20 RSV)

After this the land soon became theirs by possession. Faith had removed the final obstacle, the wall of separation, between them and the land of promise.

Jericho reminds us of the wall around which we pace restlessly and hopelessly unless we follow that latter "Joshua" and watch Him demolish that barrier of transgressions for us. That wall between us and our Promised Land falls flat before faith in Him who has melted it down with His blood. Over those ruins the children of God march victoriously into the Eternal City after their "Joshua," their Savior.

SAMUEL

Be doers of the Word, and not hearers only, deceiving yourselves.

James 1:22 RSV

More than a Hearer

Hebrews 11 and James 1 are separated by just a few pages in the Bible. Still there is a close connection between the two, for the heroes of faith listed in Hebrews are men and women who demonstrate the admonition of James: "Be doers of the Word, and not hearers only, deceiving yourselves. . . . He who looks into the perfect law, the law of liberty, and perseveres, being no hearer that forgets but a doer that acts, he shall be blessed in his doing." (James 1:22, 25 RSV)

The first time we see Samuel, he is a young boy, boarding with the high priest, Eli. When the voice called Samuel's name in the night, Samuel was told to answer: "Speak, Lord, for Thy servant heareth." From the very beginning of his life, Samuel was a hearer of God's Word. He listened carefully to every word that came to him from the mouth of God. God had listened favorably to the prayer of Samuel's mother for the gift of a son. Now that son spent his life hearing the Word of the Lord.

Hearing itself is no great achievement, though it is the

necessary starting point for a life of service to God. That life is stillborn unless the hearing produces action.

Samuel heard more than the Word of God. In all parts of the land he heard grumbling about conditions. And the people had something to complain about. Many things needed correction. Ever their religious leaders, such as Eli, left much to be desired. Privately and publicly, people expressed their dissatisfaction with things as they were. But then, as now, hardly anyone went beyond shaking his head and clucking his tongue. If a man set about to do something about the wrongs in the land, he was an unusual person. Such a person would qualify for a place on a special list of heroes. And that's where we find Samuel.

From God, Samuel had learned what a man and the people of God should be. He saw for himself what had been deformed from the image that God had made. What was needed was a drastic and thorough reformation. Many people were ready to change if only someone would get up and lead them.

To move from passive hearing to active doing is not easy or natural. Most people find it so challenging or unattractive or dangerous or lonely that they content themselves with curbstone coaching. They refuse to take a definite stand for fear of losing their safe position. Or they refrain from expressing a conviction in order to leave themselves free to criticize the people who do. Samuel could have chosen that safe and undisturbed way for himself. Eli was giving him a lesson in letting things drift as they will. There is a promise of security in keeping your neck in while the votes are being taken and waiting to see which way the majority is going.

Samuel could not and would not be satisfied with just listening. When the Lord speaks, He tells His people to *do* something, to act for Him on behalf of sinners. When worshipers rise from listening and proceed to doing, the kingdom of God moves, the body of Christ grows, the grace of God floods the land with blessing, and prodigal children of God see the signposts directing them home.

Only faith can move mountains. Only faith can move a man or a woman from hearing to doing. Samuel had it, and he moved and acted. He reformed the land which had strayed from the Lord.

And the land was cleansed. The people had reason to stop complaining. It had taken some doing. It had taken someone to do the doing. And the Lord found His someone in Samuel.

ELIJAH

I have been very jealous for the Lord, the God of hosts.

1 Kings 19:14

At the Bottom of the Barrel

Dauntless, bold, and fearless men. The world has seen many of them. They have ventured out against staggering odds to defend a cause, to liberate nations, or to make a name for themselves. Seldom, however, has there appeared in the cause of God a hero as striking as Elijah the Tishbite, who lived around 900 B.C. We must exhaust a thesarus of synonymns to adequately describe the man.

There are times when God's cause demands a fearless champion. The reign of Ahab in Israel was one such time.

Ahab was a powerful but evil ruler. Idolatry flourished in the land, and the king himself led the people in their drift away from the one true God.

Suddenly, like John the Baptist, God's latter-day Elijah, the prophet appeared in the wilderness. Having just informed Ahab that there would be neither dew nor rain for a long time, Elijah was commanded by God to hide in the desert region by the brook Cherith, and there the ravens (imagine!) would feed him. What did Elijah do with such a strange order? "He went and did according to the word of the Lord" (1 Kings 17:5). And there the greedy ravens brought bread and meat to God's man twice a day.

Soon the brook dried up. Now the prophet was subjected to another test. He was to travel to Sidon, a foreign country, and stay with a widow (imagine!) who was to feed him. Another strange command. But we read: "So he arose and went to Zarephath" (1 Kings 17:10). No questions, no excuses. Just obedience. When he arrived near the city, he found the widow getting ready to prepare her last meal for herself and her son. At the Lord's suggestion, Elijah demanded to be served the first part of this meal, and promised that the widow's food supply would not run out until the end of the drought.

Both Elijah and the widow had reached the bottom of the barrel. You may recall a certain type of children's bowl which has a picture on the bottom. You may have eaten from one yourself as a baby. The object is to get the child to eat up his cereal to see the picture on the bottom of the dish. Well, there was a picture of sorts at the bottom of the meal jar and oil cruse in the widow's house. It was an open hand of the Lord, and the legend read: "The Lord will refill." With his eyes of faith Elijah could see that picture there.

The widow, as if inspired by the faith of the prophet,

"went and did as Elijah said; and she and he and her household ate for many days" (1 Kings 17:15). Panic and fear are contagious emotions. One terrified person in a crowd can set off a stampede or plunge the entire group into despair. On the other hand, one strong and fearless person can buoy up the hopes and spirits of many others. Elijah's faith was the combustible kind that ignited others to hope and believe.

We could go on to list numerous other situations in which the stalwart faith of God's man Elijah enabled him to face the wrath and whims of a bloody dictator, saw him through a one-man-plus-God challenge of 450 popular priests of Baal, and brought him unscathed to the floor of a flaming chariot that winged him out of this life and straight into heaven! Elijah had his lapses, his moments of frustration and despondency that come to all of the Lord's mighty warriors. But these passed as the word of the Lord sought out Elijah, lifted him up, and carried him along from wonder to wonder on the glorious road of faith.

Elijah ranks with John the Baptist as a forerunner of the Savior. His preaching was a bulldozer leveling the highway for the Messiah and a broom sweeping out hearts to prepare a throne room for the King of kings.

What fan, what fanatic, what zealot of the Lord would not desire a double portion of Elijah's spirit in a world far gone in dryness and hunger, fear and evil?

ELISHA

Then Elisha prayed and said, O Lord, I pray Thee, open his eyes that he may see.

2 Kings 6:17a RSV

Believing Is Seeing

Elisha, God's bald and bold hero, seemed to have been finally backed into a corner.

The king of Syria (Ben-Hadad) was troubled because top secrets were leaking out of his palace to his enemy, the king of Israel. Tracking the leaks, he discovered it was Elisha, the prophet in Israel, who was to blame. "So he sent there [to Dothan] horses and chariots and a great army; and they came by night and surrounded the city" (2 Kings 6:14). The bird that had been chirping out the secrets was trapped—or would be without much difficulty.

Early the next morning, Elisha's servant stepped out of the house and saw the Syrian army with horses and chariots round about the city. He ran trembling to Elisha and cried: "What shall we do?"

Unruffled at this turn of events, Elisha said: "Fear not, for those who are with us are more than those who are with them." (2 Kings 6:16)

The servant must have wondered: "Is he mad? More with us than with them? How can there be? There's a whole army out there, blocking every way of escape; and there are just the two of us, a very unmilitary man of God and a terrified servant. Elisha must be seeing things!"

For a fact, Elisha *was* seeing things! What he "saw" kept him calm and unafraid. His faith had provided him with a vision of impenetrable protection. "Then Elisha prayed and said, 'O Lord, I pray Thee, open his eyes that he may see.' So the Lord opened the eyes of the young man, and he saw; and behold, the mountain was full of horses and chariots of fire round about Elisha." (2 Kings 6:17 RSV)

With his natural sight, Elisha could see no more than his servant. And to see that was enough to make any man walk out with his hands up, surrendering to superior forces. But Elisha had received a supernatural sight when he put his trust in the God of David, who had written some 100 years earlier: "I sought the Lord, and He heard me and delivered me from all my fears. . . . This poor man cried, and the Lord heard him and saved him out of all his troubles. The Angel of the Lord encampeth round about them that fear Him, and delivereth them. Oh, taste and see that the Lord is good; blessed is the man that trusteth in Him." (Ps. 34:4, 6-8)

God had placed the "fear extinguisher" near Elisha by giving him this promise of protection in the Psalms, and Elisha reached out for it and was saved in his troubles. Similar promises are situated by the loving Lord in every corner and at every turn of the believer's life. They need only to be grasped.

The fiery angels and chariots were there surrounding Elisha and his servant all night long. The Syrian army could not move in on them so long as this inner circle of divine armor protected them. The eyes of God's believing children are privileged to see protection that unbelief can never see.

To demonstrate the Lord's control of the situation, the Syrian army was stricken with blindness, and in a later siege panicked in confusion at the sound of an invisible army.

Elisha's faith found the escape hatch in that tight corner

in Dothan. He knew about it long before Paul wrote it out in 1 Cor. 10:13 RSV: "God is faithful, and He will not let you be tempted [tested] beyond your strength, but with the temptation [test] will also provide the way of escape, that you may be able to bear it."

JONAH

A man had two sons; and he went to the first and said, Son, go and work in the vineyard today. And he answered, I will not; but afterward he repented and went.

Matt. 21:28, 29 RSV

The Reluctant Prophet

Somehow God's will gets done, if not by willing servants, then by reluctant ones. Like Jonah.

The mission God assigned to Jonah was an awesome one. Nineveh was known as "an exceedingly great city." Its population of perhaps more than 600,000 was large for those days. And the entire city was so drenched in wickedness that God threatened to overthrow it unless it repented. Jonah was selected by God to take that stern and unpopular message to the foreign capital. It was not an assignment the average man of God would covet.

Jonah as much as said no to God's command. When God ordered him to go eastward to preach judgment and repentance to Nineveh, Jonah went down to the Mediterranean Sea and booked passage on a ship going west to Tarshish. The voyage was no ticket seller's mistake. Jonah was determined to go "away from the presence of the Lord." (Jonah 1:3)

The next chapter of the story is familiar to everyone. Jonah was caught short as at the end of a leash. Via the large fish God had created for this purpose, Jonah was brought back to shore.

"Then the word of the Lord came to Jonah the second time, saying, 'Arise, go to Nineveh, that great city, and proclaim to it the message that I tell you.' So Jonah arose and went to Nineveh, according to the word of the Lord." (Jonah 3:1-3 RSV)

Entering the city boldly, Jonah cried the simple message of the Lord: "Yet forty days, and Nineveh shall be overthrown!" And, to his amazement (and regret!), the people of Nineveh believed God and repented, "from the greatest of them to the least of them." (Jonah 3:4, 5 RSV)

And God spared the city gladly, delighting in its repentance.

The attitude of Jonah before and after his challenging mission cuts down his size in our eyes. And yet the mission he performed required heroism, boldness, and zeal. It is likely that Jonah learned, before God finished with him, that he himself was as much the object of God's patience and mercy as were the people to whom God sent him, and that Jonah himself needed to turn around in his flight away from God no less than the Ninevites needed to stop fleeing from God in their hearts.

At any rate, Jonah did finally say yes to the Lord's will, even though his first reaction was negative. He was like the first son in the story Jesus tells in Matthew 21: "A man had two sons; and he went to the first and said, 'Son, go and work in the vineyard today.' And he answered, 'I will not'; but afterward he repented and went. And he went to the second and said the same; and he answered, 'I go, sir,' but did not go. Which of the two did the will of his father?" (vv. 28-31 RSV). Obviously the first.

God would like to have His servants do His bidding willingly from the start; but He will settle for the latecomer who may have begun reluctantly and then did the will of the Father from the heart. Jesus assures us that there will be many "Jonahs" and "Bar-Jonas" (Son of Jonah) in the kingdom of God, while many who knew the will of the Father from earliest childhood will not enter the kingdom.

We pray: "Thy will be done on earth as it is in heaven." It is important that those who pray these words mean what they say and do that will. Although he began reluctantly, Jonah finally did that will.

Some become God's heroes because God will not take "No" for an answer.

MARY

Be it unto me according to Thy word.
Luke 1:38

A Vessel Offered to God

At one time Mary looked forward to the average life of a poor Jewish housewife. Her fiance was a carpenter, but this was no promise of wealth and luxury. If it were God's will, she would rear a family, and they would be a happy circle around their Nazareth hearth. That and little more could Mary expect when her life was suddenly and forever changed by the amazing visit of the Lord's angel.

Reaching from heaven after centuries of human history, the finger of the Lord God came to rest upon this unknown girl. Mary, of all the women in the world, would be the "blessed" one for all generations to come. In her wildest dreams she could not have imagined such honor and grace coming to her. She would be the instrument and vessel of God for the birth of the world's Redeemer! Those of low degree had been lifted up before. Mary could list any number of them in Jewish history. But who had ever been exalted like this? A Holy Thing would be born of her, a sinner! How could this be? Why should she be the mother of the Lord?

Overwhelmed by this appointment to destiny, Mary was humbled and awed. She could find in herself no reason why she should be so selected. Yet how all of a pattern this action of God is! Mary tells about it in her magnificent song, the *Magnificat:*

My soul doth magnify the Lord,
and my spirit hath rejoiced in God, my Savior.
For He hath regarded the low estate of His handmaiden;
for, behold, from henceforth all generations
shall call me blessed.
For He that is mighty hath done to me great things;
and holy is His name.
And his mercy is on them that fear Him
from generation to generation.
He hath showed strength with His arm;
He hath scattered the proud in the imagination
of their hearts.
He hath put down the mighty from their seats
and exalted them of low degree.

He hath filled the hungry with good things;
and the rich He that sent empty away.
He hath holpen His servant Israel,
in remembrance of His mercy;
as He spake to our fathers, to Abraham,
and to his seed forever. (Luke 1:46-55)

The song of Mary says many things about her.

This teen-age maiden knew her Bible. Some scholars have found as many as 24 echoes of Old Testament Scripture in her brief song. The Messiah was no stranger to this poor girl. The expectation of the Savior enriched and filled her hungry life. She knew the faithful Lord would one day perform His promise, and the world would see its Savior.

What does a person like this do when God comes with such an offer of glory? She has nothing to offer but herself as a willing vessel of God. "Behold the handmaid of the Lord; be it unto me according to Thy word."

Was there ever another person in history like Mary, so blessed, so sought out by the Lord, so chosen to be His vessel? Her Son and God's Son says: "Who is My Mother? . . . And He stretched forth His hand toward His disciples and said, Behold My mother and My brethren! For whosoever shall do the will of My Father which is in heaven, the same is My brother and sister and *mother.*" (Matt. 12:48-50)

By the grace of God, Mary became the vessel of God and bore God's Son within her. By God's grace there are many Marys, equally precious to Him and equally honored by Him, who offer themselves to the Lord and are filled with His salvation. Blessed Mary! Blessed mothers of the Lord!

THE WISE MEN

Where is He who has been born King of the Jews?
Matt. 2:2 RSV

Wise Men in Search of a King

All the preparations had been checked and double-checked. Each of the distinguished travelers was ready. They would leave together the very next day. The caravan would be equipped for a long journey. It might be months before they returned, if they could be sure of returning at all. Travel was dangerous in those days, especially for wealthy people.

But they were determined to go anyway. They didn't know how far they would be traveling. That would be up to the star. It had appeared in the heavens, and it was on the move. Westward.

They were known as wise men. But, to all appearances, they looked foolish setting out after a moving star, like simpletons pursuing the rainbow to find the pot of gold at its end. They might not look so wise if their calculations proved to be wrong. They would look quite silly coming back home, poorer but much wiser. They could still change their mind and stay home. They could let the star go on without them.

But were their calculations off? They had done their research painstakingly. They had followed carefully the directions of the most reliable guide they could find. There it had been written: "There shall come a Star out of Jacob, and a Scepter shall rise out of Israel" (Num. 24:17). This meant that the arrival of a great king would be marked by a special star. In their study of the skies they recognized the new star and made their decision. They would seek out the King whose coming was proclaimed by the heavens. They counted themselves fortunate to be living when this long-awaited event was taking place. Hundreds of years before, their ancestors had heard about the One who was to come for the Jewish nation, then captive. Daniel and his countrymen had boldly and openly proclaimed the true God who would someday send the world its Messiah. Somehow this prophecy had gotten into the hands of the Wise Men, and now they were about to have a part in the great drama.

They were more that just curious about what was happening. They had more than an objective scientific interest in the heavenly phenomenon. They were sure that the Dayspring (the Morning Star) from on high was about to visit mankind sitting in midnight darkness. The appearance of the star convinced them that the ancient promise was true. The Creator of the star was sending the newborn King. They were prepared to kneel before Him, Baby that He was, and worship Him.

There was no more time to lose. Their houses must be set in order before their departure. Someone must take charge of their affairs while they are gone, and take over for them should they not return. And gifts had to be prepared, royal gifts, for the infant King. No detail was overlooked.

The journey began. Finally they arrived in Jerusalem. Straight to the palace they went and asked their question: "Where is the King?" Not: "Is there a King?" but, "Where is He who has been born King of the Jews?" It wasn't the right place. That nameplate belonged not in Herod's palace, but over a stable and later on a cross. But they were on the track. There was such a King. They would just have to travel a little farther before they found Him. The exact place of His birth was Bethlehem, not Jerusalem. A slight correction in their directions, another look at the star, and they were on their way.

Yes, they would find Him. The seekers would locate the Seeker, and both would be happy to have found each other.

THE WIDOW OF THE MITES

She of her want did cast in all that she had, even all her living.

Mark 12:44

More than an Offering

The call to worship has sounded. In homes throughout the city, young and old of every class are preparing to visit the Lord's house. First the dressing up in the best clothes, then the calling together of the family, then a last look around that nothing has been forgotten. Oh, yes, remember to take along an offering!

In one of those homes, a poor one, a lonely widow is going through the same preparations. She may stop to wonder whether she should go this day at all. She is down to her last two mites. Together, the two coins are hardly worth picking up off the table. They can scarcely purchase a sacrifice to be offered in the temple by the priest. Besides, there would be other worshipers in the temple who would be better dressed than she. Out of their surplus they would be able to contribute more than she has to her name. She could certainly use those two mites for her own needs. Tomorrow the stores would be open again, and she would be hungry. She could buy a little food with the mites, enough to make a last meal before she would be completely dependent on others.

But she was "hungry" now, and the temple of God was open. There she could picture the Bread of Life waiting to feed her, and the Water of Life which satisfies. Had not God said: "Man shall not live by bread alone, but by every word that proceedeth out of the mouth of God?" (Deut. 8:3). Sooner or later she would have to invest those two mites in food, and then they would be gone. Suppose she decided to give up that food and make a last sacrifice instead. Had not God been opening His hands to feed her until now? It would be little enough to show Him how much she appreciated His goodness and trusted Him for the next day's cares.

Who knows what she thought, the nameless widow of the two mites, as she closed the door of her house and walked up Zion to the temple? We might as well imagine that she went through no mental torture trying to decide how much of an offering to contribute that day or whether to go to church at all. For all we know, her casting of all her money into the treasury may have been done all in one motion as part of a life moving with everything it has in the direction of God.

The widow may not have known it, but she was involved in a crucial decision. Not only the rich are tempted by money. So are the poor. The rich are inclined to make it everything in their life because they have it. But the poor can make it everything in their lives too, simply because they do not have it and are always worrying about it. The rich man can delude himself into thinking that he has done all that is necessary if he has given something to God and to charity. And yet the giving may not have deprived him of any comfort or luxury or caused him any loss. The poor man, on the other hand, may excuse himself from doing anything at all in the way of service to God or his fellowman by pleading poverty, as if to say: "You prevented me from doing anything, Lord, because You made me so poor."

At offering time in the service, the widow's mites outranked much larger sums falling into the treasury that day. Many of the others were merely leftovers; hers was a sacrifice. In the church treasurer's books her coins hardly made it to the decimal point. But in God's book they put many others to shame.

JOHN THE BAPTIST

I tell you, among those born of women none is greater than John.

Luke 7:28 RSV

None Greater

Many in the days of Jesus were making big headlines in the world. Roman emperors were shaping events and nations. Writers were recording for the ages immortal prose, poetry, and drama. Sculptors were fashioning masterpieces in stone. Architects were designing structures that awe us to this day. The military were forging invincible forces.

Scientists were busy making far-reaching discoveries. Doctors and philosophers were gaining new insights into the body and mind of man. It was a rich and lively age. Some even left their names in history as men and women who knew how to outdo all previous generations in devising special pleasures.

And in a desert, next to a crooked river running through a corner of the world, a young man, about 30 years old, was gathering crowds of curiosity-seekers to hear his strange message: "Make straight the way of the Lord" (John 1:23). It was a peculiar message from a peculiar man. He was dressed in camel's hair, and he fed on locusts and wild honey. The message contained more. He pointed to Jesus passing by and cried: "Behold the Lamb of God, who takes away the sin of the world!" (John 1:29 RSV)

His ministry did not last long. His scene on the stage of history was brief. It was cut short when he criticized the puppet king of Palestine, was thrown into prison, and then was beheaded during the king's wild birthday party. A few of John's followers buried his body, and that would have been the last trace of him, except . . . except that Jesus said: "I tell you, among those born of women none is greater than John."

He must have had reasons for saying so. We all have our measurements for greatness. Some use the yardstick of power or accomplishments or beauty or service or the number of lines a celebrity rates in *Who's Who*. Wouldn't it be interesting to know how God measures greatness?

A few of His standards come readily to mind: "He [God] delighteth not in the strength of the horse; He taketh not pleasure in the legs of a man. The Lord taketh pleasure in them that fear Him, in those that hope in His mercy" (Ps. 147:10, 11). "To this man will I look, even to him that is poor and of a contrite spirit and trembleth at My Word" (Is.

66:2). "You know that the rulers of the Gentiles lord it over them, and their great men exercise authority over them. It shall not be so among you; but whoever would be great among you must be your servant, and whoever would be first among you must be your slave; even as the Son of Man came not to be served but to serve, and to give His life as a ransom for many." (Matt. 20:25-28 RSV)

John lived by the motto: "He [Jesus] must increase, but I must decrease" (John 3:30). To him, Christ was the Bridegroom, he himself was just one of the attendants at the wedding. The finger of his life and words was not pointed at himself, but at Him whose shoelaces John did feel worthy to untie. John knew that "He who comes from heaven is above all" (John 3:31). He was determined not to diminish the light of God's Son by letting the shadow of his own personality stand in front of it. When people were looking for their life and their peace, he would not permit his head to be in the way. He would lower himself so they could see Jesus standing above him.

It looks as if we must revise our list of history's greats. The mighty men of old will have to step down and let this "prophet" occupy the first place. "A prophet? Yes, I tell you, and more than a prophet. This is he of whom it is written, 'Behold, I send My messenger before Thy face, who shall prepare Thy way before Thee'"(Luke 7:26, 27 RSV). This very last herald of the Savior, Jesus places at the head of the list.

But this isn't the end of the sentence. The whole of it goes like this: "I tell you, among those born of women none is greater than John; yet he who is least in the kingdom of God is greater than he." That could be you—Or I!

THE TENTH LEPER

Then one, when he saw that he was healed, turned back, praising God with a loud voice; and he fell on his face at Jesus' feet, giving Him thanks. Now he was a Samaritan.

Luke 17:15, 16 RSV

In Sickness and in Health

A hero of World War II distinguished himself valiantly in battle. After the war, as a civilian, he lost the battle of the bottle. In war he was a hero, in peace, a failure.

In their dreadful illness 10 lepers had learned to pray and where to look for help. As Jesus came by, they cried to the Lord of might and mercy: "Have pity on us." Who wouldn't pity the poor wretches? Separated from health and family and society, they lived a living death. No malady was more dreaded in those days than leprosy. Only rarely was it cured. Most victims could expect to remain lepers until they died. No wonder the lepers who caught Jesus passing by near them begged Him to have mercy on them.

And Jesus answered their prayer, providing them with the precious gift they desired: normal health.

Suddenly the need for Christ vanished. He was a foulweather friend, and they had just stepped out of the storm into the sunshine of glowing health. There was so much lost time to make up, so many things to do. They hurried off in all directions, each to resume his own life. Now they could get along without Jesus. Who needs a doctor when he isn't sick? They would keep Him in mind if they possibly needed Him again.

One of them, however, stops in his tracks, looks again at his restored body, blinks his eyes in amazement, and immediately turns around to locate the Giver of this precious gift. All the rest can wait. He has a debt to repay, and a mere thank-you will hardly do. But he must at least say thanks.

The man has no name. But he does have a tag. He is a Samaritan. And this makes his reaction all the more unusual. It was normal behavior for Samaritans to look down or askance upon the Jews. And Jesus was a Jew. Anything the Jews had, the Samaritans felt they could match or exceed. They wanted to owe nothing to the Jews, from whom they had separated centuries before. The "normal" Samaritan reaction to Jesus would have been: "Take what He can give you, but don't lower yourself before Him, don't place yourself under obligation to Him." We are impressed by the Samaritan's response because he overcomes this impulse to behave in a normal Samaritan manner.

Besides, he overcomes the hazard of good health. Sickness makes pray-ers and beggars out of many who would not otherwise turn their thoughts upward. It is easy to do without God when one's body is functioning perfectly. One can go for years without feeling the need of God, and since good health seems to be a sign that all's well with the world, feelings of guilt do not seem to send the healthy person hunting for a Savior.

The healed lepers were still sinners even though their health was restored. The granting of health was not a sign that their sins were forgiven. They were still creatures of God even though they were no longer outcasts of the community. And the fact that they were members of God's chosen race made them no less needful of the Messiah whom God was sending the world through their nation.

But all this seemed normal. They felt they had this coming to them. They would have felt cheated if they didn't have this normal life. After all, didn't others enjoy good health and spiritual blessings without getting down on their knees each day to beg for them?

The Samaritan ex-leper met the test of health as well as he met the test of illness. He passed the test of prosperity as well as he passed the test of adversity. In sickness and in health, his faith stayed anchored in the same Rock.

"He turned back, praising God with a loud voice." If he could cry out in misery, could he keep silent in joy? "And he fell on his face at Jesus' feet, giving Him thanks." Who else deserved the credit for making him whole?

Jesus, seeing this one-out-of-ten response, said to him, "Rise and go your way; your faith has made you well" (Luke 17:19 RSV). The other nine were still sick with a fatal illness. This one was healed forever.

THE SYROPHOENICIAN WOMAN

Then Jesus answered her, O woman, great is your faith!

Matt. 15:28 RSV

A Treasure Not to Be Lost

Usually Jesus is pictured in the Scriptures as the Seeker. He is the Good Shepherd hunting for the one lost sheep. He is the King sending all His messengers into the highways and byways to invite all to His great supper so that every single remaining place at His table is occupied. No one can mistake His personal interest in every human being, an interest so intense that each can say, "Christ died for *me* and gave Himself for *me*."

On one occasion, however, our Lord seems to step out of character. We find Him retiring for a while in the foreign regions of Tyre and Sidon. There "He entered a house and would not have anyone know it; yet He could not be hid (Mark 7:24 RSV). He wished to remain incognito, for reasons not revealed. But He could not be hid, any more than a candle on a stick or a city on a hill. Especially to someone who was searching for Him as diligently as was the Canaanite women of Syrophoenicia.

Pleading for her demon-possessed daughter, she came to Jesus. She knew Him to be more than a passing charlatan, a fly-by-night faith healer. She called Him by a name that acknowledged Him for what He was: the Son of David. And she called Him Lord. Put these two names together and you have the equivalent of Messiah, or Savior. It was the Savior, coming from the nation and lineage of David, in whom this Canaanite woman was putting her trust for help. She knew that He would be able to cast the devil out of her child, for He had come into the world to destroy the works of the devil.

It is here that we run across one of the strangest remarks ever heard from the lips of the loving Savior. "I was sent only to the lost sheep of the house of Israel." It was as though He were deliberately brushing her off. But she would not be discouraged. She made her way past the circle of disciples, who resented being pestered by her. Like a puppy at the heels of her master, she kept coming, begging for attention. "Lord, help me!" she cried.

Again Jesus answered: "It is not fair to take the children's bread and throw it to the dogs." He meant that the feast of salvation was prepared on the table of the

Jewish nation. Their seats were set around the table first. The Savior had come to their race, to their land, spoke their language, and bore the name of their God, Immanuel. Still the woman would not be put off. She came back with the reply: "Yes, Lord, yet even the dogs eat the crumbs that fall from their master's table."

The woman had caught sight of a treasure to be coveted, something so rich that it overflows the table on which it stands. It was already in the hands of God's chosen people, but she desired some of it too. She didn't want it taken away from them to be given to her; she would be satisfied with the leftovers.

Jesus, in delaying His response to her, was testing her hold on the treasure. How much did she really want it? Would ridicule later make her release her grasp of it? Suppose people said to her: What do you want with that Jewish salvation? Our Phoenician culture and religion are superior or at least every bit as good. Why do you lower yourself to associate with those people who once tried to wipe out our ancestors?

She stayed with the test till it was over. She kept knocking at the door of the Kingdom which is for all, Jew and Gentile alike. When Jesus saw her confirmed in her decision, He welcomed her with a rare sentence of commendation. He who can detect faith the size of a mustard seed said to this woman: "Great is your faith!"

She had persisted long enough to learn that "everyone who asks receives, and he who seeks finds, and to him who knocks it will be opened." (Matt. 7:8 RSV)

LYDIA

If you have judged me to be faithful to the Lord, come to my house and stay.

Acts 16:15 RSV

The Best Purple Anywhere

The world of business can be a dangerous arena. It is filled with victims who have been scarred in cutthroat combat with ruthless competitors. Certain ventures on that battlefield end in ulcers, dishonesty, scandal, or even death. The stakes are high, the ground rules are tough, and the casualties are legion.

In that agitated arena stood a certain woman named Lydia, a native of Thyatira. She was a seller of purple, an expensive textile, in the city of Philippi. All indications hint that she was a successful career woman.

Her brief biography in Acts 16 states that she was also a worshiper of God. Today that would be nothing unusual. Many business people are members of the church. But then, in Philippi, it was worth remarking that Lydia was both a businesswoman and a worshiper of the true God. As difficult as it is to be both today, a merchant and a consistent believer, it was more difficult then.

The entire city was pagan. People who did not worship the gods of the Greeks stood out among the majority. And merchants who were not pagans were even more conspicuous. In fact, they were asking for a hard struggle.

JONAH—"Thy will be done on earth as it is in heaven."

The heathen merchants were wary of competition as it was, but they were particularly on guard against nonpagan competition. It was in that very city that Paul and Silas were framed and jailed by the owners of a slave girl who became a Christian because of their preaching, and who stopped making money for her owners by fortunetelling. Lydia dared to be a merchant and a worshiper of God under those circumstances.

Running into such obstacles, Lydia might have felt that she had done enough to have made a gesture in the direction of religious affiliation. She might have felt it wise to play down her church connections and gradually to push her faith into the background. She could turn to it if she had to. Or she might exploit her religious ties to get a few Jewish and Christian customers. But she did none of these things.

Rather she made her position more hazardous by opening her heart to the Gospel and being baptized a Christian. The circle in which she was enclosed now grew smaller still. There were at least more Jews in the city than Christians, and if the Jews had only the pagans against them, as a Christian she would have both the pagans and the Jews boycotting her store. But this did not stop Lydia either. She proceeded to have her entire household baptized, and then she opened her home to the apostles as a church.

There is no record of her having abandoned her career at this point. Instead she converted it, too, into a calling and used it to serve the Lord and her fellowmen. She, who knew the value of purple goods, discovered the priceless value of the garment of righteousness woven of crimson strands on the loom of the cross. She knew that the wearer of that "purple" would be marked as a royal priest before God. Not only she herself could now wear this garment, but her customers and friends, admiring it, would desire to have one like it themselves. And she could tell them where to get it, not wholesale, but completely free of charge.

Prior to her conversion, Lydia could offer the Philippians the finest quality of goods, patrician purple. Now those who came to her store could find there the best "purple" anywhere.

SIMEON

Lord, now lettest Thou Thy servant depart in peace, according to Thy word.

Luke 2:29

Standing at the End of the Line

Many of God's heroes appear in their young and vigorous years. They show their faith in a heroic feat or burst of action under tremendous odds. Their very youth makes them impatient with the past and with the *status quo*. They can hardly wait to correct the mistakes made by their forefathers. So heroism is often the medal on a young man's chest.

However, not all of God's heroes were pioneers or trailblazers. Some, like aged Anna and Simeon, stood at the end of the line, growing old as they waited for the fulfillment of God's promises. Their confidence does not appear in the divine record as the explosion of a supernova in the skies, but as a steadily glowing star, flickering its light night after night in the world's deep darkness. This is

not easy. Most would prefer the single bold action to the long, long wait. Simeon waited and waited and waited.

The Bible pictures Simeon as that just and devout man in Jerusalem "waiting for the Consolation of Israel." "And it was revealed unto him by the Holy Ghost that he should not see death before he had seen the Lord's Christ." (Luke 2:25, 26)

God had made a rare promise to Simeon. Thousands upon thousands before him had the same hope of seeing with the eyes of their flesh the fulfillment of God's great promise of salvation. Simeon was one of the rare, blessed ones whose eyes were privileged to witness the Lord's first coming. "Blessed are the eyes which see what you see!" Jesus told His contemporaries. "For I tell you that many prophets and kings desired to see what you see, and did not see it, and to hear what you hear, and did not hear it" (Luke 10:23, 24 RSV). God promised Simeon that he would be one of those fortunate persons.

One day it finally came about. That day the Spirit of God led Simeon to the temple (what better place to find God's promised Word?) and while he was there, a poor couple, people of the working class, entered, carrying a Baby. Simeon approached them, took the Child into his own arms, blessed God, and spoke the Nunc Dimittis: "Lord, now lettest Thou Thy servant depart in peace, according to Thy word, for mine eyes have seen Thy salvation." (Luke 2:29, 30)

Now his life was complete. He had arrived at the point for which he had been born and loved by God, and for which God had prepared His Salvation. He was through

SIMEON—". . . flickering its light night after night in the world's deep darkness."

waiting. Now he could depart in peace. In his arms he held the cancellation of all his debts, the fulfilling of all his deficiencies, and all the light that he needed to cross the black river of death. There, in a little bundle, was the love and Word of God made flesh. It could be held and embraced, received and treasured. It could be seen and felt. It was real. It was worth waiting for, no matter how many long and dreary years.

With this experience another word of Christ applied to Simeon: "The last shall be first, and the first last." Seemingly at the end of the line of Old Testament waiters, Simeon is one of the very first in the line of New Testament witnesses of the Savior. And he is in the lengthy glorious list of God's heroes as proof that God's promises are fulfilled for those who wait Him out.

JOHN

Hereby perceive we the love of God, because He laid down His life for us; and we ought to lay down our lives for the brethren.

1 John 3:16

Thunder and Love

"Boanerges" Jesus nicknamed John and his brother James. "Sons of Thunder" was a fitting description of the two at the time they were called to be disciples. Even after they had been following Christ for a while, the flashes of temper were still there. When a village of Samaritans would not welcome Jesus, their Master, James and John said to Jesus: "Lord, wilt Thou that we command fire to come down from heaven and consume them, even as Elias did? But He turned and rebuked them and said, Ye know not what manner of spirit ye are of. For the Son of Man is not come to destroy men's lives but to save them." (Luke 9:54-56)

James and John were not only impatient. They were driven for a time by a consuming ambition to lord it over others, to acquire the first and second places in the coming kingdom of Christ. Their mother backed them up in this request, interceding for them before Jesus. Though the Lord admired zeal and persistence in people, He would not coddle or excuse anger and ambition in His disciples.

As John (and his brother) stayed on with Jesus, he came more and more under the Lord's warming influence. By and by, Boanerges was no longer an apt picture of John's nature. Eventually that name was replaced by the enviable appellation "the disciple whom Jesus loved." The zeal was still there, but it was no longer squandered in short-fused blowups. Now it was channeled into the steadily flowing exercise of love. Of all the disciples John became the closest to Jesus. This was inevitable as he resembled more and more the nature of his Lord.

Faith meets many challenges. One of the most difficult, so as to be almost impossible, is to love others. Love is the fulfilling of the Law, the performance of God's will. And we know that no one can do this to the complete satisfaction of God. Our keeping of the commandments breaks down in the area of love. To be able to love perfectly would be to be equal with God, for God is Love. The more godly a person becomes, the more loving he is. Love distinguishes between the believer and the unbeliever, between the saved and the lost, between true godliness and hyprocrisy. Without love, even dying for one's faith and feeding the poor and being expert in religious knowledge are worth nothing. (See 1 Cor. 13)

Love is truly a difficult virtue. It borders on the heroic, especially when it reaches out to embrace one's enemy and prays for one's persecutor. Love is just as difficult to exercise within the family, between children, between children and parents, and vice versa. There must have been family squabbles in John's family in their early years, what with the quick tempers and the competition for supremacy. But this gave way as love took over. John must have learned the power and technique of love from Christ very well. He was the logical one to be entrusted with the care of our Lord's mother Mary as Jesus died on the cross. And it isn't too hard to imagine Mary in her declining years catching frequent glimpses of her divine Son in John as she saw love growing and glowing in him.

To John, this part of Christian faith was to be valued most highly. His letters exalt the love of God in Christ and urge the reader to reflect God's love in all human relations.

As John increased in love, he soared higher and higher and moved in the lofty companionship of God. The eagle is a good symbol for John. The disciple of love was blessed with special insight and depth and visions, and lived in the closest possible communion with his Lord.

It's a long way from thunder to love—but faith can bridge the gap. It did for John.

BARTIMAEUS

And Jesus said to him, Go your way; your faith has made you well.

Mark 10:52 RSV

". . . The Blind See . . ."

Bartimaeus was accustomed to being silenced. People eventually got tired of hearing him plead for alms. It didn't help to throw him a coin one day. He was there with his hand outstretched again the next day. Blind Bartimaeus could hear some footsteps making a wide circle around his roadside station. He could almost sense them turning away their eyes so that they would not have to see the sightless wretch. It spoiled their day to find this blotch of abnormality sitting in their workward or playward or homeward path. If only he would keep quiet and resign himself to his fate! Who could help him? No doctor was known to cure such ailments. He was stuck with his tragedy. If he would just stop inflicting his misery on others, stop making them feel guilty and helpless.

Now once again "many rebuked him, telling him to be silent." It was embarrassing for the multitude striding along with Jesus out of Jericho to have the town's beggar disrupting the mood. "But he cried out all the more: 'Son of David, have mercy on me!'" (Mark 10:48). He couldn't keep quiet this time. Jesus was passing by! He had to catch the ear of Jesus. This was the only Person who could help him. And He might not come this way again. "Jesus, Son of David, have mercy on me!" came the wail from his hoarse throat.

And Jesus heard. Bartimaeus knew it was really Jesus by the way He responded to the cry. Jesus stopped and said: "Call him." His heart began to pound faster as he was told that Jesus was calling him. How like the Jesus he had heard so much about! Merciful, kind, sympathetic. At least He cared enough to stop.

Bartimaeus threw off his mantle at once, jumped up, and groped his way to Jesus. Now the tension was almost unbearable. Then Jesus spoke again: "What do you want Me to do for you?" It couldn't be true. This was too much like a dream. Would he dare to open up his heart to Jesus?

What did Bartimaeus want of Jesus? Not money. Others could give him that. He needed much more than money. "Master," he said, "let me receive my sight." It was the prayer of every blind man, woman, and child since blindness first visited mankind. It is a prayer that always touches the soft heart of God and of His Son. But this particular prayer went deeper than the surface cry of despair and longing. Underneath it Jesus found something more. "And Jesus said to him, 'Go your way; your faith has made you well.'" (Mark 10:52)

Bartimaeus had seen in Jesus more than the sighted multitudes around Him. John the Baptist had sent his own doubting disciples to Jesus to ask Him if He was the Messiah who was to come or if they should wait for another. Jesus sent back the message: "Go and tell John what you hear and see: the blind receive their sight and the lame walk . . ." (Matt. 11:2-6). By this miracle the multitude with Jesus would be able to identify Him for what He was. Unfortunately they saw in Jesus, going to Jerusalem and His crucifixion, the son of David, royal descendant of their once great and glorious king, but not the Son of God, the Only-begotten of the Father, full of grace and truth. They saw in Jesus their potential emancipator from Roman military occupation, not the Redeemer who had come to destroy the works of the devil and to break the bondage of sin.

Bartimaeus found the mercy of the Savior, and it covered more than his sins. It removed for him the blindness of his eyes. He was one of those who were literally sitting in great darkness and saw a great Light.

PETER

Jesus immediately reached out His hand and caught him.

Matt. 14:31 RSV

The Fallen Can Stand Too

Does the life of a drowning person flash before him as he sinks for the last time? Who knows? Yet the story of Peter's faith-life is captured in that miraculous water-walking experience of his on the Sea of Galilee.

Peter and the other disciples were rowing hard against the wind late at night. Suddenly the Lord Jesus appeared to them, walking on the water. To make sure it was not a ghost, Peter challenged the figure: "Lord, if it is You, bid me come to You on the water." The answer was, "Come!" "So Peter got out of the boat *and walked on the water.*" Look! He could do the seemingly impossible! He could imitate the Son of God!

The miracle did not last long, however. When Peter saw the wind lifting the waves around him, he faltered and sank. On his own, the weight of his human nature pulled him down. And "Jesus immediately reached out His hand and caught him, saying to him 'O man of little faith, why did you doubt?'" (Matt. 14:28-31 RSV)

Later again it was nighttime, and Peter tried once more to do what seems humanly impossible: he tried to remain loyal to the Lord while trusting in his own strength. He had felt pretty sure of himself. "Even if I must die with You, I will not deny You," he promised Jesus. But the waves of suspicion, ridicule, possible imprisonment, even martyrdom, rose to threaten him in the questions of the servants around the campfire. Peter, losing sight of his Lord and seeing just the waves, began to sink. Before the rooster crowed twice, Peter was going down for the third time.

He looked up then, and there was the Lord. All he could do was cry in his heart to the Savior: "Lord, save me!"

Then came Easter and the reinstatement on the shore of Galilee. Jesus was reaching out His hand again to poor Simon. He was still nearby, only a look and a call away. On the shores of that very sea Peter had heard His voice invite him: "Follow Me, and I will make you a fisher of men." Now He was saying: "Feed my lambs . . . Feed my sheep." Again the impossible. Would Peter make it this time?

He didn't have to wait long to find out. One day the court that had condemned Jesus to the cross was asking Peter: "Do you know this Man?" Now Peter did not falter or hedge. The reply was strong and clear: "There is salvation in no one else, for there is no other name under heaven given among men by which we must be saved"

PETER—". . . the Lord Jesus appeared to them, walking on the water."

(Acts 4:12 RSV). Back in the courtyard of Caiaphas, Peter had been terrified that the servants had seen him with Jesus. Now, in the court of Caiaphas, "when they saw the boldness of Peter . . . they recognized that [he] had been with Jesus" (Acts 4:14). Now Peter corroborated the suspicion of his Lord's enemies with a fearless confession.

Now Simon was living up to the name Christ had given him, "Rock-man." He had discovered that to be solid he needed to stand upon the Rock of Ages, upon "that living Stone, rejected by men, but in God's sight chosen and precious," a cornerstone laid by God. (1 Peter 2:4-7 RSV)

Peter had learned that "it is better to trust in the Lord than to put confidence in man." Mindful of his failures because of self-confidence, he wrote in his First Epistle: "God opposes the proud, but gives grace to the humble. Humble yourselves therefore under the mighty hand of God that He may exalt you in due time." (1 Peter 5:5, 6 RSV)

This was something to remember when he stood before his own cross. Even there the Hand was outstretched to uphold him.

THE CENTURION

Truly, I say to you, not even in Israel have I found such faith.

Matt. 8:10 RSV

Table Space for a Foreign Soldier

The streets of Capernaum, our Lord's headquarters during His Galilean ministry, often shook to the thunder of marching feet. The city near the Sea of Galilee harbored a Roman garrison. It was not at all unusual to run into soldiers and officers anywhere in town.

The Jews, whose country was occupied by the mighty Romans, had learned to live with the situation, as much as they resented it. And the soldiers, because of their special mission, had little to do with the Jews, whom they despised. Prejudices against foreigners and minorities were as strong then as they are today.

The Lord, however, drew no boundary lines. He had come to seek and to save that which was lost. And all were lost, Jew and Roman alike. He came to bring light to those sitting in darkness. And all were in darkness. He came to bring life to the dead. And all were "dead in trespasses and sins." He came to reconcile those who had become God's enemies and had lost His peace. And all were captives of the devil until Jesus took captivity captive.

Somehow a centurion, a captain in the Roman army, learned this about Jesus. And through his uniform, through his alien nationality, the grace of God penetrated, and his allegiance was shifted to a higher Ruler. This soldier found salvation among the Jews and even built a synagog for them in Capernaum.

This centurion is a remarkable man in many ways. He represents one of the early trophies won by Christ out of the pagan world. His faith is demonstrated by one virtue after another. Instead of the expected callousness of the typical Roman soldier (such as those who tortured and mocked Jesus before His crucifixion), this officer was moved by love and sympathy for his servant, of all people! The servant was likely a Jew. At any rate, to the ordinary Roman he was just a slave, a piece of property. One didn't usually waste sympathy on slaves or become disturbed by their suffering. Slaves were meant to suffer. But this centurion contradicts all expectations. He is sorry for his paralyzed and suffering servant. He wants to do everything he can to help him.

The centurion searched out Jesus and pleaded with Him to do something for the servant. He calls Jesus "Lord." Here was another break with his pagan background. If anyone was lord to a Roman, it was one of many gods, or the emperor. To the centurion, Jesus of Nazareth, of the despised Jewish race, was the Lord. This is not just a title of respect, but a recognition of Jesus as the Savior. The centurion believed that Jesus could do for him and his servant what neither Roman gods nor emperor could do. Besides, he felt unworthy in the presence of Jesus. Something must have changed in him: a Roman unworthy in the presence of a Jew!

"The Jews seek a sign," says Paul, analyzing a peculiar characteristic of his people. But so do many others who demand some special evidence that the power of God is operating. The centurion brushed aside all such crutches for his faith. He said: "Lord, I am not worthy to have You come under my roof; but only say the word, and my servant will be healed. For I am a man under authority, with soldiers under me; and I say to one, 'Go,' and he goes, and to another, 'Come,' and he comes, and to my slave, 'do this,' and he does it" (Matt. 8:8, 9 RSV). This kind of faith Jesus had never before witnessed. "When Jesus heard him, He marveled and said to those who followed Him, 'Truly, I say to you, not even in Israel have I found such faith.'"

And then He pointed to some empty chairs that are set around the King's table in heaven, and said that they would be occupied by people like the centurion from the east and the west, and they would sit next to Abraham, Isaac, and Jacob. It was wonderful when the Jews who were anticipating the Messiah for centuries recognized Him when He came and believed in Him. But when a Gentile soldier had eyes to see the Lord's Christ, this was enough to make Jesus Himself marvel!

THE SINFUL WOMAN

She loved much. Luke 7:47

No More Imitation Love

The invitation stated, "Dinner is served at the appointed hour." Jesus presented Himself at the door of the Pharisee's house, entered, and sat down at the table.

The meal had just begun when a woman with a bad reputation in town came into the house uninvited, holding in her hands an expensive jar of perfume, and weeping. In shocked silence the host watched what she did next. She came behind Jesus and let her tears fall on His feet. Then she dried them with her hair and anointed them with the perfume. Speechless, the Pharisee thought: "If this man were a prophet, He would have known who and what sort of woman this is who is touching Him, for she is a sinner." (Luke 7:39 RSV)

For all his close watching, the Pharisee saw only a corrupt woman polluting his house with her presence, imposing on his hospitality. Besides, he was a little disappointed in Jesus. He had considered Jesus a prophet, a preacher of righteousness, a man who holds virtue and godliness in high regard. All at once he felt he was the holiest one in the room. He did not see that he and the woman were both in need of the same thing, the thing both of them were seeking and for which they were finding only substitutes.

Like everyone else, the Pharisee and the woman were looking for love. They wanted to be loved. But they were mistaken about love. They were accepting substitutes and counterfeits. The Pharisee confused love with recognition and praise. He wanted others to think highly of him, including Jesus. He was even willing to spend the price of a dinner to obtain this kind of approval. His paying for that approval was calculated. He felt the dinner invitation was enough for now. There was no need for him to greet Jesus enthusiastically or to offer Him a basin of water to wash the dust off His feet. He would invest no more in this dinner than he had to. There was the possibility that Jesus might let him down.—And He surely did.

The woman had also been looking for love for a long time, perhaps since childhood. Many women with her kind of reputation are desperately clutching at any semblance of love. They, too, are often deceived by imitation love. They think it can be found in a function of the body, an emotional thrill, a flattering word. But what she peddled and what others bought was not love after all. The fairy tales and novels and popular songs called it love, but it was really something else. The love she knew was also calculated and bartered and paid for in one way or another.

One day the sinful woman, who had in her way "loved" much, met Him who loved genuinely, divinely. He had nothing to gain for Himself by offering her the love of God. One day those feet she was washing and kissing and anointing would be nailed to a cross for her many corruptions. Here was love, not that she had loved God, but that God had loved her and gave His only Son to be the atonement for her sins.

She found love when she found Jesus, for Jesus

showed her the heart of God, which is love. The more she saw of that love, the more grateful she felt, and the more she loved God in return.

The Pharisee held on to his counterfeit love, which was really a love of himself. He felt little need for forgiveness, and none for faith in his holy Guest. And so he loved little.

The bad woman found love when she found forgiveness, and she found both when she found Christ. By these steps she crawled out of the gutter into the clean and holy and happy family of God: by Christ, by forgiveness, by faith, and by love. Such people go into the kingdom of God ahead of the Pharisees.

PAUL

"I know whom I have believed."
2 Tim. 1:12

"I Know!"

You see something happen. It happens to you. It seems unbelievable. Someone asks you to prove what you are reporting. What do you do? Whatever you do, you say, "It is so! I know!" Eventually the argument has to stop. There is no rebuttal to "I know!" except the cruel accusation "You must be out of you mind. It cannot be!"

Paul heard this kind of remark and insinuation many times after he saw the Lord Jesus on the road to Damascus. Especially when he placed the miracle of Jesus' resurrection before people. And yet, what else could he do? He had seen the risen Jesus with his eyes. And the sight had turned him around in his tracks.

Before the vision, Paul was Saul, a self-righteous, zealous persecutor of the Way and of those who walked the Way. Then Saul felt no need for a Savior. Jesus was superfluous. In fact, Jesus was a threat to the monument Saul was building of his own life, inscribed SAUL. Jesus was someone to kick out of the way, even if you hurt your toes doing so. He was competition for the current ruler of Saul's heart and life, that is, Saul.

Now all this was changed. And the point of change had been that vision of the risen crucified Lord Jesus saying: "Saul, be My special messenger." Eventually, that is what Saul became. With the change of his outlook and goal came a new name, Paul. And Paul was a new man, radically different from the old. Paul saw the miracle of a new birth take place within himself. And he knew *who* caused it, not *what* caused it. It wasn't a question of reform, for the former Pharisee felt no need for reform. He thought he was perfectly acceptable to God as he was. It was simply this: Paul had been turned to God by having his feet set upon Him who is the only Way to the Father.

To Paul it was simple, a miracle, and a fact. But to those to whom he testified, the miracle was madness.

Faith cannot be scientifically investigated or described. It amounts to trusting in the unlikely, the unseen, the impossible. When Paul talked about Jesus, he was publicizing someone who could not be seen, whose body was not even around to check. When Paul explained that Jesus was God's Son, this was brushed off as unlikely. Of

PAUL—". . . the miracle of a new birth takes place within himself."

course, they would go along with the idea of a Supreme Being, but that this Supreme Being should have a Son who enclosed Himself in a human body, this was not only unlikely, it was preposterous. And to become even more fantastic: that this Man, crucified according to ancient prediction, died, was buried, and rose from the dead! This could be accepted only by faith.

All Paul could say was, "I know!" There were no doubts in his mind about it. He needed no scientific proof, he did not have to put his hands and fingers into the side and hands of Christ's body. He knew!

And because he knew what Christ was and what He had done, Paul knew what was waiting for him beyond the grave. "I know whom I have believed, and I am sure that He is able to guard until that Day what I have entrusted to Him" (2 Tim. 1:23 RSV). That's faith, when you can say, "I know!"

Such believers know the blessedness Jesus means when He says: "Blessed are they that have not seen and yet have believed." (John 20:29)

THE PENITENT MALEFACTOR

Jesus, remember me when Thou comest into Thy kingdom.

Luke 23:42

Just, Just in Time

Don't be surprised to find faith just about anywhere—except in hell. In a child, in a dying old man, in a king or a beggar, in a soldier or a merchant, in a tax collector or a prophet, in a fallen women or a pious matron. Even in a criminal hanging on a cross, a few gasps from death.

Two thieves, traditionally named Dysmas and Testas, were crucified with Jesus on Good Friday. Dysmas had only to glance to his left to see the suffering Man nailed to the center cross. And looking above the Man's head, he could make out the accusation posted in mocking title: JESUS OF NAZARETH, KING OF THE JEWS.

Strange, no one was treating this Jesus like a king. Rather He was being mistreated as though He were the greatest criminal on Golgotha. From the moment He was cruelly nailed hand and foot to the accursed tree, the bystanders, from rulers and priests to soldiers and rabble, railed at Him. Even Testas was drawn into the ghastly game. Dysmas could understand that he and Testas deserved such treatment, but there was nothing in the center Man to merit such torture. Why, He wasn't even worthy of death!

Gradually Dysmas began to see in Jesus more than a bruised and bloodied remnant of a man. He heard Jesus praying for His crucifiers! He saw Him bearing the cross and its shame without cursing. This kind of meekness and love stood out in that setting of violence and hatred. More than that, Jesus was mockingly being called the "Son of God." That was the answer! All of it made sense if Jesus was really the Son of God. The superscription on His cross was true: Jesus was the King, not only of the Jews but also of the everlasting kingdom of heaven. That crown of thorns made His crown of glory more splendid. Those scars in His hands and feet were proof that God is Love and that He has no pleasure in the death of the wicked, but that the wicked should turn from his way and live. And that blood trickling down that body and cross—the blood of

God's Son—could cleanse him of all his sins. For that was the Lamb of God being sacrificed for Dysmas and the world before his very eyes!

Dysmas believed. And just in time. In a few hours the last chance to return to his heavenly Father would have vanished forever. There was no time left to make up for a lifetime squandered on himself. But all that he needed was on that center cross. How near and how adequately and how opportunely the love of God reaches out to the sinner! Glancing to the left, he could see the door to the Father's house ajar the width of a cross, just wide enough for him to squeeze through and into the light beyond.

"Jesus," cried Dysmas. The name of salvation was first announced in a night turned into day by the brightness of many joyous angels. Now it is spoken in a day turned into night by the sins of many creatures. Calling upon that name in faith saves. Dysmas called upon it and was told: "Truly, I say to you, today you will be with Me in Paradise." (Luke 23:43 RSV)

Dysmas saw in Jesus the only One who could save him even so late. And Jesus saw in Dysmas a brand to be snatched from the burning. He extended to the lifelong sinner the robe of sainthood washed white in His own blood.

The faith of Dysmas was not just adequate. It was extraordinary, considering the circumstances. He not only confessed his utter unworthiness, but he acknowledged Jesus to be the King of heaven. He counted on Jesus to perform everything necessary for his redemption. And he even tried to do a little mission work with his newfound faith. By publicly confessing his faith in Jesus and reproving the other criminal for his sins, he was witnessing to the Lord.

The malefactor's faith shines still brighter when we see

it in its gloomy Good Friday setting. As yet there was no Easter on the calendar to confirm his faith. But for him the dying Lord on the center cross was victorious already, and Easter was certain to take place. He wanted an appointment in heaven with the Lord he expected to find there alive in glory.

Dysmas moved from the right hand of grace to the right hand of glory in a few moments. For many a wrong-doer that journey covers many years, and some miss the glory because they scorn the grace. Dysmas arrived safe at his goal. He saw his last chance and caught his Savior's hand just in time.

TIMOTHY

A disciple was there named Timothy, the son of a Jewish woman who was a believer; but his father was a Greek.

Acts 16:2 RSV

Beating the Handicap of Birth

Young Timothy gave no indication of being the mixed-up child of a mixed marriage.

He might have been. His believing mother and pagan father might have agreed at his birth that the child should be let alone in respect to his religious upbringing. They might have said, "Wait until he is older, then let him decide for himself what he wants to believe. As for now, we won't mention the subject."

And the child, seeing one parent interested in religion and the other lukewarm or indifferent, might have become confused as to what to believe or whether to believe in anything at all.

By the grace of God, Timothy escaped this spiritual disaster. Normally, in an all-Jewish household it was the responsibility of the father to bring up his children in the nurture and admonition of the Lord. God had prescribed for Israel that in this way His commandments, precepts, and promises should be transmitted from generation to generation. When Timothy's pagan father defaulted in this task, Eunice, his mother, and Lois, his grandmother, took over the basic religious training of the child.

As early as possible they set his little feet on the paths of righteousness and placed into his tiny hands the lamp to light his path. Paul reminded Timothy of this maternal influence in his life when he wrote to his pupil: "From a child thou hast known the Holy Scriptures, which are able to make thee wise unto salvation" (2 Tim. 3:15). Instead of the ephemeral wisdom of the Greek philosophers, Timothy was imbued with the wisdom exalted by Soloman and embodied in Jesus Christ. "The Greeks seek after wisdom; but we preach Christ Crucified: unto the Jews a stumbling block and unto the Greeks foolishness; but unto them which are called, both Jews and Greeks, Christ the Power of God and the Wisdom of God" (1 Cor. 1:22-24). In the Scriptures, Timothy had found the wise will and plan of God for him and for all men in Christ.

Since Timothy had no spiritual father in his own home, St. Paul became Timothy's "father," begetting him as a child of God by the seed of the Gospel. The elder statesman of Christ liked to think of Timothy as his "own son in the faith," his "dearly beloved son." Now Timothy belonged. Now he was adopted into the very family of God. Now he could grow and flourish normally without the handicap of fractured emotions. His life was anchored and secure.

When his other assistants proved unreliable, Paul could turn confidently to Timothy to carry on the work he had begun. Writing to the Philippian Christians from his imprisonment, Paul gave Timothy this lofty endorsement: "I hope in Jesus Christ that it will not be long before I can send Timothy to you. . . . I have nobody else with a genuine interest in your well-being. All the others seem to be wrapped up in their own affairs and do not really care for the business of Jesus Christ. But you know how Timothy has proved his worth, working with me for the Gospel like a son with his father." (Phil. 2:19-22 Phillips)

Timothy kept growing stronger and stronger in this loyalty to the cause of Christ. According to tradition, Timothy, as an elderly bishop in Ephesus, was confronted one last time with the power and pressure of Greek paganism. According to tradition he was killed while attempting to stop an indecent heathen procession during the festival of Diana.

From beginning to end he was all Christ's.

DORCAS (TABITHA)

She was full of good works and acts of charity.
Acts 9:36 RSV

"Now There Abideth . . . Charity"

"The evil that men do lives after them, the good is oft interred with their bones," was the cynical remark of grief-stricken Mark Antony at the death of Julius Caesar, according to Shakespeare. It isn't necessarily so. There is the case of Dorcas (or Tabitha), a certain follower of Jesus who lived in Joppa in the days of the apostles.

Good as she was, Dorcas had died, as everyone must. Considerately, her friends took care of the funeral arrangements. They laid out her corpse in an upper chamber until the hour of burial.

As the news of her death spread through the community, many gathered to pay their respects to the woman eulogized by the Bible as "full of good works and acts of charity." When it was learned that Peter was at nearby Lydda, he was called and arrived at the house, where "all the widows stood beside him weeping and showing coats and garments which Dorcas made while she was with them" (Acts 9:39 RSV). Her friends were poorer by one good person, and a large quantity was subtracted from the supply of love in the world. The death of Dorcas was a great loss to those who were left behind.

Dorcas died, but the good that she had done went on living after her. It was like seed planted to bear fruit later. Like the coats and garments she had made for the poor, the coverings of love she had woven during her lifetime were still warming the chilled and lonely souls of many. She had been a fountain of kindness. Yet more amazing than the sudden shutting off of that fountain was the emergence of that fountain in the first place.

Dorcas was not just a certain woman living in Joppa, who happened to be a very charitable person. She is recorded for all time as a certain *disciple*. That meant that she was a follower, or pupil, of the Lord Jesus. This was the

DORCAS—". . . well of living water . . . which flowed forth to enrich lives of others."

well of living water which had sprung up in her and which flowed forth to enrich the lives of others.

Love is something that comes from God, who is Love. No one produces it by himself. "If we love one another, God dwelleth in us, and His love is perfected in us" (1 John 4:12). "We know that we have passed from death unto life, because we love the brethren. He that loveth not his brother abideth in death" (1 John 3:14). God permitted Dorcas to be raised from the dead by Peter, in order for her to go on loving for a while longer, not in order to pass into life. She had already passed from death to life when she was raised from selfishness to service by her faith in Jesus Christ. She was alive for God because she followed Jesus. That was why she loved her fellowman.

She was raised from the death of the body in that upper chamber. It was in an upper room that Jesus showed His disciples how they could demonstrate the risen life He had come to give them. There He took a towel and girded Himself and washed the feet of His disciples and said to them: "Do you know what I have done to you? You call Me Teacher and Lord; and you are right, for so I am. If I then, your Lord and Teacher, have washed your feet, you also ought to wash one another's feet. For I have given you an example, that you also should do as I have done to you." (John 13:12-15 RSV)

Dorcas had learned the meaning of discipleship. It consists in following, following Jesus obediently, following Him in trust, following Him in love and in sacrifice, following Him through death into life eternal with the Father. Dorcas was that kind of disciple. There were the coats and garments to prove it.

STEPHEN

And they stoned Stephen, calling upon God.
Acts 7:59

Killed in Action

Some soldiers never get to see the Purple Heart they have won for heroism. They die as they earn the award. The medal is given to their families after their death.

In the long list of martyrs in the New Testament age, Stephen stands as the first Christian "killed in action." At the climax of his heroic defense of the faith, a volley of stones fell upon him as he knelt praying the prayer of his Lord: "Lord Jesus, receive my spirit." "Lord, do not hold this sin against them." Stephen did not live to see the far-reaching effect this loyalty to the end had upon the infant church.

Stephen was not a pastor. He was a layman in the Jerusalem congregation of the Christian church. In the course of time he had been appointed to the office of deacon. His duty was to see that the widows of the Greek Christians were not neglected. As he performed this office, Stephen was practicing the "pure and undefiled religion" described by St. James (1:27). This meant visiting the widows and fatherless in their affliction and keeping himself unspotted from the world. This kind of religion is for every Christian to practice, pastor and layman alike. Stephen was a model of it. And he backed up his charity work with persuasive testimony so that those who disputed with him "could not withstand the wisdom and the Spirit with which he spoke." (Acts 6:10 RSV)

No one quarreled with Stephen's charity work. It was with the latter "plus" that he ran into trouble. Stephen's fault, as they saw it, was not that he had an inner conviction about Christ, but that he dared to be vocal about it. But Stephen felt that he had a confession to make, and he was going to make it. For it was this faith that had changed his life and made him truly concerned about the poor and neglected people. It was this faith that had brought him, orphaned and wretched in sin, into the bliss of the heavenly Father's family.

Though his critics kept on harassing Stephen, they failed to silence him. They would have to resort to more forceful means. So a group of them secretly instigated some false witnesses to bring a charge of blasphemy against Stephen before the council. Now this was the same accusation that was laid to Jesus before the very same Sanhedrin. At that time, too, the high priest expressed amazed indignation at the accused standing before him. All around him Stephen could see men who, as Jesus had said, "devour widows' houses and for a pretense make long prayers" (Matt. 23:14). Stephen stood before them, his face like that of an angel. The council ranged about him, gnashing their teeth at him in rage. The contrast continues to the very end. Stephen stood gazing into heaven, his eyes glistening with the vision of the Son of God standing at the right hand of God. They cried with a loud voice as they stopped their ears and rushed together upon him, cast him out of the city, and stoned him.

There Stephen fell to his knees, praying the prayer of forgiveness his Lord had prayed for these same people. "And when he had said this, he fell asleep." (Acts 7:60)

If medals were given for this type of bravery and loyalty, they would have to be awarded to Stephen's heirs (in this case, the church, us) posthumously, and they might very well be inscribed with the words of Heb. 11:38: "Of whom the world was not worthy."